IN PROFILE

Women Prime Ministers

Richard Gibbs

SILVER BURDETT

In Profile

First published in 1981 by
Wayland Publishers Ltd
49 Lansdowne Place, Hove
East Sussex BN3 1HF, England

© Copyright 1981 Wayland Publishers Ltd

Adapted and Published in the United States by
Silver Burdett Company, Morristown, N.J.

1982 Printing

ISBN 0-382-06638-3

Library of Congress Catalog Card No. 81-86273

Phototypeset by Direct Image, Hove, Sussex
Printed in the U.K. by Cripplegate Printing Co. Ltd.

Contents

Sirimavo Bandaranaike

Sirimavo Bandaranaike became the world's first woman Prime Minister in 1960, after the assassination of her husband. Her ambitious socialist policies proved unpopular and her government was defeated in 1965. Returning to power in 1970, she was defeated again in 1977, following allegations of corruption, fraud and the misuse of power. Three years later she was stripped of all her civic rights.

Sirimavo Bandaranaike came to power in Sri Lanka in July 1960, a few months after the assassination of her husband. The tragic death of Solomon Bandaranaike, who had ruled as Prime Minister for three years, shocked the island. He had been worshipped by thousands of Ceylonese peasants who saw him as a crusader for freedom and democracy. Suddenly his grief-stricken widow found herself thrust into the whirlpool of Sri Lankan politics.

Sirimavo Bandaranaike had never played an active role in politics, but she felt that she had to carry on the work her husband had started. Summoning up all her reserves of courage, she vowed that if she were elected Prime Minister she would carry out the programme of reforms to which her husband had dedicated his life.

Thus it was that in July 1960 she led the Sri Lankan Freedom Party to a decisive victory in the general election, and Sirimavo Bandaranaike became the world's first woman Prime Minister.

Sirimavo Ratwatte Dissawa was born on 17th April 1916, at Balongoda in Sri Lanka, or Ceylon as it was then known. She had four brothers and two sisters. Her father, Barnes Ratwatte Dissawa, was a powerful Kandyan chief, and was descended from a line of nobles that had ruled the island until it was conquered and colonized by the British in 1802. Sirimavo's

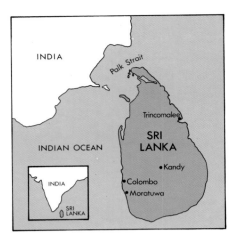

The island of Sri Lanka, previously known as Ceylon.

Solomon Bandaranaike and his wife in 1956.

mother also came from an aristocratic background. The family lived in a beautiful mansion, with spacious gardens, servants, and an abundance of good food.

The family was well-liked and respected by the island's poverty-stricken villagers. Her mother was a skilled practitioner in Ayurveda—a form of traditional healing—and gave freely of her time to tend the sick. Sirimavo's father was a benevolent chief who taught his daughter to respect principles of tolerance, fair play and justice.

At an early age, Sirimavo went to stay with her aunt at Ratnapura, so that she could attend the Ferguson Primary School. Her schoolfriends remember her as being a studious, quiet girl who, unlike most of them, was not at all afraid of the dark, spiders, snakes or 'creepy-crawlies'.

Sirimavo marries

When she left primary school, Sirimavo went to St. Bridget's Convent School in Colombo, the capital of Sri Lanka. Colombo was an important port and the centre of the British colonial administration. Although life at the convent was fairly sheltered, Sirimavo came into contact with a wide range of Western influences in the city. She became proficient in English and read a great deal of English literature.

Sirimavo grew up to be a beautiful young woman and attracted the attentions of many young men. One of them, who came to court her on numerous occasions, was Solomon West Ridgeway Dias Bandaranaike. He too came from an aristocratic family and had studied at schools and universities in England.

Solomon Bandaranaike was an ardent nationalist and a radical socialist. He was a member of Parliament and leader of the Sri Lankan Freedom Party. Sirimavo's father did not approve of his

Voters queue outside a polling station near Colombo.

politics, but the young couple had fallen deeply in love and he gave his blessing to the marriage.

Sirimavo Bandaranaike became a devoted wife and mother. She had no political ambitions and concentrated on bringing up their three children.

At this time, her husband was involved with the nationalist movement, which was dedicated to achieving self-rule for Ceylon. In 1947, the Labour Government in Britain finally granted Ceylon independence. Solomon Bandaranaike and his Sri Lankan Freedom Party lost the first elections to the United National Party. The U.N.P. was backed by British capitalist interests and for nine years the island saw little change.

Ambitious reforms

Bandaranaike was swept into power in 1956. He immediately embarked on an ambitious programme of reform. Wages were increased and workers were given their rights. He expelled the British army and navy from their bases on the island and established diplomatic relations with Russia, China and other Communist countries.

Mrs Bandaranaike remained on the fringes of political activity. She was hostess at 'Temple Trees', the official residence of the Prime Minister, where she entertained and came into close contact with many world leaders and Ceylonese politicians. She also visited a number of foreign countries with her husband and accompanied him to important conferences.

Solomon Bandaranaike—despite his aristocratic background—was a man of the people. He was the hero of the oppressed peasants and workers, and was always keen to hear the opinions and complaints of ordinary men and women.

Every morning he would hold open house to listen

7

Solomon Bandaranaike lies in state after being shot in September 1959.

to the views of his countrymen and explain the policies of his government. The lack of security at these meetings did not concern him, as he felt it more important to be a leader who was accessible to the people.

On the morning of 25th September 1959 tragedy struck. A Buddhist priest walked into the house and fired six shots at the Prime Minister at point blank range. Sirimavo ran screaming to her husband's side, but he had died instantly.

Prime Minister of Ceylon

The tragic death of Solomon Bandaranaike stunned the island. Thousands of illiterate peasants—whose cause he had championed—came to pay their last respects to the man who had been a symbol of their hopes, and offer their condolences to his grief-stricken widow.

Solomon's death came as a severe blow to the Sri Lankan Freedom Party, which he had helped to create, and which now found itself without a leader. Officials of the S.L.F.P. decided that Sirimavo Bandaranaike was the only person capable of uniting the disparate elements within the party. They implored her to accept the position of leader of the party and to carry on the work her husband had started. She accepted the challenge.

During the next few months she managed to unite the warring factions within the party and addressed more than 900 election meetings all over the island. In the general election of July 1960 she led the S.L.F.P. to victory, despite an intensive Press campaign against her.

On the day she was officially named as Prime Minister, Sirimavo Bandaranaike returned home to a house crowded with relatives, friends and well-wishers who had come to offer their congratulations.

She walked in silence through the crowd and went to the place of honour in the house where her husband's picture hung. There she prostrated herself before his image and said a silent prayer, asking for guidance in the challenging task that lay ahead of her.

The country she had been chosen to lead faced formidable difficulties. It was very poor and largely dependent on foreign aid. There were tensions between the majority Singhalese people and the Tamils who had arrived from India centuries ago to establish a kingdom in the northern part of the island. This tension had erupted into violence on numerous occasions in the past.

In her first major speech to the country, Mrs Bandaranaike stressed that her government would pursue the socialist policies of her late husband. Singhalese was declared the official language of the country. She also announced an ambitious programme to develop the health services, improve housing, modernize agriculture, reduce food prices and take over control of the schools from religious institutions. Large areas of government land were to

Many of the poor in Sri Lanka can only survive by begging on the streets.

Mrs Bandaranaike with her cabinet in 1960.

The Sri Lankan Parliament in Colombo.

be made available for development by landless peasants, and grants would be made available to enable the poor to develop trade, agriculture and cottage industries.

Mrs Bandaranaike committed her government to a policy of non-alignment in foreign affairs. This meant that the country would act independently of the major power blocs. She also announced that the government would introduce legislation to take over the country's major newspapers.

Intense opposition

As well as being Prime Minister, Sirimavo Bandaranaike was also Minister of Defence and External Affairs and Minister of Information and Broadcasting.

She and her government faced intense opposition during her first five years of power. The Buddhist clergy were incensed at her decision to nationalize their schools. The Tamils were angry because Singhalese has been made the official language of the country. Powerful business interests, represented by the conservative United National Party (U.N.P.), fought her socialist programme every step of the way.

In the elections of 1965, Mrs Bandaranaike's government was toppled by the U.N.P. By now the country was in the throes of a serious economic crisis: unemployment and the cost of living were rising and there was an acute shortage of consumer goods.

The new Prime Minister, Dudley Senanayake, made concessions to the Tamils which eased tensions, relaxed state controls of industry, and succeeded in securing Western foreign aid. Mrs Bandaranaike, now Leader of the Opposition, headed a United Front composed of the S.L.F.P. and a minority of Communist and Trotskyist M.P.s.

From Prime Minister to political outcast

*Returns to power . . .
Violent rebellion . . .
Suspends civil
liberties . . . Ceylon
declared a Republic
. . . Motion of No
Confidence in Parlia-
ment . . . Suspends
Parliament . . .
Opposition to
nationalization plans
. . . Dissolves Parlia-
ment . . . S.L.F.P.
defeated in 1977
elections . . . Retains
seat . . . Allegations
of corruption . . .
Found quilty . . .
Banned from holding
public office.*

In 1970, Mrs Bandaranaike was returned to power by a large majority. Her government promised reforms as it had done before. But the pace of change was slow, and the peasants and large numbers of young people, suffering from the effects of unemployment, became increasingly restless.

A year after coming to power, the country erupted into violent insurrection. Armed left-wing groups tried to seize power in a bloody coup in which 1,200 people were killed. The rising was crushed by the army and police. Sixteen thousand people were detained without trial and civil liberites were suspended.

Mrs Bandaranaike was severely criticized but she managed to ride out the storm. In May 1972, Ceylon was declared a Republic and from then on was to be called by its traditional name, Sri Lanka. Five thousand detainees were released, but the Tamil Federal Party boycotted the ceremonies. They were demanding greater use of the Tamil language, which was spoken by twenty per cent of the people.

The following five years imposed a severe strain on Mrs Bandaranaike. The country's expectations had been raised by her promises of reform, but Sri Lanka was still extremely poor and money was needed to bring about the changes she had promised—money the country did not have. The peasants continued to live in desperate poverty, and the severe shortages of food and other essential commodities led to violent protests. Mrs Bandaranaike was accused of corruption and of granting favours to her son Anura, a member of Parliament.

In February 1976, the Opposition proposed a motion of No Confidence in the government. She suspended Parliament in order to prevent large sections of her party from supporting the motion. The Communist Party announced that it was withdrawing its support from the government and a large number of

The Minister of Transport salutes a group of Buddhist monks. They are a powerful force in Sri Lanka.

left-wingers in her own party resigned.

A year later, in an attempt to win back the support of the Left, Mrs Bandaranaike announced plans to nationalize all British banks and all land controlled by religious institutions. After fierce protests, however, she said the plans would be delayed for a while. She dissolved Parliament and began preparing for the election which would take place in July 1977.

Mrs Bandaranaike's plan to nationalize the massive landholdings owned by the powerful Buddhist clergy caused deep resentment. Buddhist monks had exercised a powerful influence on the island ever since they first arrived in the third century B.C. The Sri Lankan Freedom Party had relied heavily on the votes of Buddhist monks during previous election campaigns. This large and influential group now felt threatened by Mrs Bandaranaike.

The weeks prior to the election were a time of feverish activity for Mrs Bandaranaike. The United National Party had embarked on a vigorous election campaign as had the Socialist Front, which was a combination of Communists, Trotskyists and disaffected left-wingers from the S.L.F.P. Mrs Bandaranaike was convinced, however, that she would win the election despite the formidable opposition.

But the electorate was in the mood for change, and her party was soundly thrashed. The U.N.P. had won

Mrs. Bandaranaike prepares notes for an election speech.

the biggest majority in Sri Lanka's history. Mrs Bandaranaike managed to retain her seat, but her majority was slashed by half. There had been predictions that there might be serious violence after the election, but calm prevailed.

The new Prime Minister, Mr J. R. Jayewardene, announced that a Parliamentary Commission would be set up to investigate allegations of fraud, misuse of power, corruption and nepotism by Mrs Bandaranaike. Three years later the Commission delivered its verdict: guilty on all counts.

Mrs Bandaranaike was stripped of all civic rights and banned from holding any public office. This shrewd woman, who had exercised tremendous influence on the country's affairs during her twelve-year reign as Prime Minister, was now cast out into the political wilderness. She defended herself vigorously, claiming that the charges against her had been 'trumped up' by her opponents, and declared she would fight the bans imposed on her by every possible means. Despite the fact that Sirimavo Bandaranaike is a born fighter, her chances of making a political comeback now seem extremely remote.

Dates and events

1916   Sirimavo Ratwatte Dissawa born in Balongoda, Ceylon (17th April).

1940   Marries Solomon Bandaranaike.

1947   Ceylon granted independence. Sri Lankan Freedom Party (S.L.F.P.), led by Solomon Bandaranaike, loses election to United National Party (U.N.P.).

1956   Bandaranaike elected Prime Minister.

1959   Solomon Bandaranaike assassinated (25th September).

1960   Sirimavo Bandaranaike leads S.L.F.P. to victory in general election.

1965   Government defeated by U.N.P.

1970   Bandaranaike returned to power.

1971   Popular uprising in protest at unemployment and social problems leads to suspension of civil liberties.

1972   Ceylon declared a Republic to be known as Sri Lanka.

1976   Opposition proposes motion of No Confidence in government.

1977   S.L.F.P. defeated at general election. Bandaranaike accused of fraud and corruption—found guilty and banned from public office.

Golda Meir

Golda Meir—'the grandmother of Israel'—was a powerful force in the campaign to create a homeland for the Jews. After the creation of Israel in 1948 she became Minister of Labour and then Foreign Minister. In 1969, at the age of seventy, she was elected Prime Minister. She led her country for four years during one of its most dangerous periods, until ill-health forced her to retire. She died in 1978 after a serious illness.

Golda Meir—'the grandmother of Israel'—dedicated her life to the birth of a new nation and its struggle for survival. It was a nation she was destined to lead through one of the most dangerous periods in its violent and bloody history. The story of this wily and courageous woman, who became Prime Minister of Israel at the age of seventy, reflects the tragic history of the Jews.

Golda Meir first went to Palestine as a young woman. It was the fulfilment of a dream she had had from an early age—to return to the ancient homeland of her ancestors and help in the creation of the State of Israel—a sanctuary for the oppressed Jews of the world. In this she was successful, but thousands of lives were lost in the struggle and wars and acts of terrorism have plagued the country since its birth.

Golda Mabovitch was born in Kiev, Russia, on 3rd May 1898. Her father, Moses Mabovitch, was a carpenter. But he was a Jew which made it difficult for him to find work. There was never enough food, warm clothing or heating for the family. Like other Jewish families in Russia and other parts of Europe, they lived under the constant threat of oppression.

One of Golda Meir's earliest and most vivid memories concerns the persecution that the Jews suffered: 'I must have been very young, maybe only

Grand Avenue West, Milwaukee.

One of the many families who emigrated to America from Europe.

three or four . . . and I can still recall quite distinctly hearing about a pogrom that was to descend upon us . . . I knew it had something to do with being Jewish and with the rabble that used to surge through town, brandishing knives and huge sticks, screaming 'Christ-killers', as they looked for the Jews and who were now going to do terrible things to me and my family . . . Above all, I remember being aware that this was happening to me because I was Jewish which made me different from most of the other children in the yard. It was a feeling that I was to know again many times during my life . . . the fear, the frustration, the consciousness of being different and the profound instinctive belief that if one wanted to survive, one had to take effective action about it personally.'

The Promised Land

As a young girl, Golda learned how Moses had led the Children of Israel out of Egypt into the Promised Land—the land that the Bible called Canaan. There they lived in freedom for 2000 years until in A.D. 70 the Romans invaded Canaan, forcing many Jews to flee their homeland. From then on Canaan was known as Palestine.

To escape persecution, many Jews fled to different parts of the world. They were an intensely religious people and wherever they went, they took their faith and customs. But the Jews were always a minority in the countries where they sought refuge. Many of them were forced into slavery or made to live in squalid conditions as third-class citizens. The one thing which gave them hope was their religion and the thought that one day they might return to the home of their ancestors.

At the age of seven, Golda and her two sisters, Zipke and Sheyna, emigrated to America with their

Theodor Herzl (1860-1904), the founder of Zionism. He convened the first Zionist Congress in 1897.

mother. Moses Mabovitch had gone there three years earlier and was eager for his family to join him.

Golda's arrival in America marked the beginning of a new and exciting period in her life. Although the Jews were a minority in America, they were not persecuted there. At last the family was free from the burden of fear they had endured in Russia. Golda went to school in Milwaukee where her parents had opened a grocery store. She was exceptionally intelligent and learned to speak English very quickly.

Golda runs away from home

She wanted to go to high school so that she could study to become a teacher. But her parents refused to let her, so she ran away from home and went to live with her sister, Sheyna, in Denver. She was determined to continue her education there.

Sheyna's home was a popular meeting place for Jewish intellectuals and Golda would listen with rapt attention to the discussions about the plight of the Jews in Europe where they suffered much persecution. She became interested in the Zionist movement which had been established in Europe in 1897. The founder of Zionism, Theodor Herzl, believed that the only solution to the persecution of Jews lay in the establishment of a national homeland in Palestine. The Zionist philosophy attracted a great deal of controversy. Many Jews said it was blasphemy and that they should wait for God to lead the Jews back to the Promised Land in his own time.

In Europe the First World War was raging. Golda became an active member of a number of organizations that raised money for homeless Jewish refugees. One day, she heard that forty Jewish men had been shot in her home town in Russia. They had been accused of spying. Golda was shocked and felt broken apart inside. Had her uncles been among

Golda Meir with children from a kibbutz.

those murdered?

From then on, her beliefs solidified into a single purpose. There had to be a Jewish homeland, a place where Jews could live in dignity and free from persecution. Golda made up her mind that as soon as she had finished high school she would save enough money to travel to Palestine and help to bring about a Zionist state.

She joined the Labour Zionist Party and toured the country making speeches and raising money for the movement.

The Balfour Declaration

During the First World War, Britain gained control of Palestine and other territories in the Middle East. In 1917 the British Foreign Secretary, Lord Balfour, declared that Britain viewed 'with favour the establishment in Palestine of a national home for the Jewish people'. The Balfour Declaration gave tremendous encouragement to the Zionists. But the Palestinian Arabs were shocked at this 'act of treachery', as Britain had previously promised independence to the Arabs. The Middle East tragedy was born. The Palestinian Arabs, who formed more than ninety per cent of the population, feared that the Jewish settlers, who began arriving in large numbers, would gain political and economic control of the country.

A month after the Balfour Declaration, Golda married Morris Myerson. He was a shy and sickly young man. Like Golda, he had come to America from Russia, but he did not share her passionate interest in Zionism. He tried to dissuade her from going to Palestine, but Golda was headstrong and committed to her dream of helping to create a Jewish state. On 23rd May 1921 the young couple sailed from New York for the Promised Land.

lucky. Thousands who came within a few miles of the 'Promised Land' were turned back.

In February 1947, two years after the end of the Second World War, Britain announced that she would withdraw from Palestine and hand over responsibility for the country to the United Nations. This was a signal for both Jews and Arabs to intensify their efforts to gain control of the country. Violence increased and there were atrocities on both sides.

In November 1947 the United Nations voted in favour of the partition of Palestine, with separate areas for the Arab and Jewish states. The Jews accepted this arrangement. The Arabs declared an all-out war, but their divided ranks were no match for the Haganah—the underground Jewish Army.

Golda Meir was again sent to America to raise money for the Haganah. Her mission was extremely successful, and within weeks she had managed to raise $50 million.

At this point Golda Meir undertook one of the most dangerous assignments of her life. She was asked by the Jewish leadership to go and meet King Abdullah of Jordan to discuss his attitude towards the State of Israel which would come into being in a few weeks.

The Knesset in Jerusalem, Israel's single-chamber Parliament.

Golda Meir in Moscow while serving as the first Israeli Ambassador to the U.S.S.R.

Golda had to travel in secret to Amman, the capital of Jordan. First she bought an Arab woman's costume and practised walking in the long skirts and trying to see through the dark veil. She and a Jewish man who was fluent in Arabic then travelled to a town on the River Jordan, where they were met by the King's chauffeur.

The journey to Amman was tortuous. The car was stopped ten times, flashlights were shone into their faces, and identification papers were demanded.

Declaration of Independence

The meeting with the King proved fruitless. Although he expressed his sympathy for the plight of the Jews, he made it clear that there seemed no way of avoiding the impending Arab war against the Jewish state. After an eventful return journey, Golda rushed back to Tel Aviv to report on her meeting and to prepare for the ceremony that would mark Britain's withdrawal from Palestine and the creation of the Jewish State.

At 4 p.m. on 14th May 1948, Golda Meir—together with the other Jewish leaders—signed the historic Declaration of Independence. Tears flooded down her face and her hands shook with uncontrolled emotion. Her dream, the dream of thousands of Jews, had come true at last.

A few days later, Golda Meir was again sent on an urgent mission to the United States to raise more money for the Jewish Army. Seven Arab nations—Egypt, Jordan, Syria, Lebanon, Iraq, Saudi Arabia, and the Yemen—had declared their intention' of driving the Israelis into the sea. The Arab armies were defeated nine months later. The Israelis, armed with weapons bought with the money Golda Meir had raised in America, had fought with grim determination to maintain their new state.

Mrs Meir with Harold Wilson (left) and Willy Brandt at the 1969 Socialist International Congress.

Golda Meir heard the news of the Israeli victory in Moscow where she had been posted as Israel's first ambassador to the U.S.S.R. A few months later she returned to Israel to take up her apppointment as Minister of Labour.

It proved to be one of the most rewarding and challenging periods of her career. Five hundred thousand Jews had fled from Arab countries to settle in the new state after Israel became independent. There were even Jews from India and China. These people needed homes and jobs; schools, hospitals and roads had to be built. Golda Meir applied herself with energy and enthusiasm to this mammoth task. In June 1956 she was appointed Foreign Minister—the second most important post in the government.

In the following years, Israel came under intense pressure to stop the bombing raids against the Palestinian refugee camps in neighbouring Arab states. Golda Meir vigorously defended her country's right to defend itself against attacks by Palestinian guerrillas.

Prime Minister of Israel

In 1965 Golda Meir announced that she was retiring from public life. She was nearly seventy years old, her health was poor, and she wanted to spend more time with her grandchildren. Her new-found tranquility did not last long, however. In February 1969 the Israeli Prime Minister, Levi Eshkol, died.

On the 7th March 1969 the Central Committee of the Labour Party voted Golda Meir the new Prime Minister of Israel. She was dazed at the news, and tears rolled down her cheeks. 'I knew that now I would have to make decisions every day that would affect the lives of millions of people, and I think perhaps that is why I cried,' she recalled years later.

Prime Minister of a war-torn nation

Israel beset with problems . . . War of Attrition with Egypt . . . Cease fire . . . Attacks on refugee camps in Lebanon . . . Israel withdraws from Lebanon . . . Olympic atheletes murdered . . . Tours world meeting heads of state . . . Receives American aid . . . Israel seizes Arab lands in Yom Kippur war . . . Uneasy ceasefire . . . Criticism for handling of war . . . Retires from politics . . . Dies.

Golda Meir faced a daunting challenge as Prime Minister of a country beset with problems. The Israeli economy was in a bad state and the country was dependent on massive loans from the United States to keep it on its feet. Defence spending was consuming almost half the budget. Inflation was getting out of control and the country was in a state of almost perpetual war.

Her first action as Prime Minister was to tell her military secretary that she was to be informed immediately of any military action, even if it was in the middle of the night.

Israel was engaged in the so-called War of Attrition with Egypt. In 1967 the Israeli forces had mounted a full-scale attack on Syria, Jordan and Egypt. Vast chunks of territory were annexed. The Arab armies suffered a humiliating defeat. But the Arab spirit had not been broken and assaults on Israel continued. However, in 1970 a cease-fire with Egypt was concluded and, for a while, the hostilities decreased.

In February 1972 Mrs Meir ordered an assault on the Palestinian refugee camps and guerrilla bases in Lebanon, following raids on Israel. The Israeli forces inflicted a severe blow on the Palestinians, and hundreds of Palestinian guerrillas were killed. Innocent women and children were also killed in massive bombing raids.

The United Nations Security Council unanimously adopted a motion demanding that Israel should withdraw her forces. Israel had no choice but to comply. The Palestinian guerrillas, however, vowed to carry on the fight against Israel. Aircraft were hijacked and Israeli embassies attacked. Then in 1972, Palestinian guerrillas kidnapped and murdered Israeli athletes at the Munich Olympic Games. The world was shocked at this savage act of terrorism and Israel retaliated by inflicting raids on Arab territories. Peace seemed doomed.

The bodies of the murdered Jewish Olympic athletes arrive back in Israel.

Golda Meir toured the world speaking to heads of state in many different countries. She repeatedly insisted that Israel wanted peace with her neighbours, but she would not budge on the question of the Palestinian refugees.

In April 1973 Israel was again condemned by the United Nations for her 'repeated military attacks' on Lebanon. Golda Meir replied that she had no option but to defend herself. She pointed out that Egypt and other Arab states were constantly violating the ceasefire. Once again Israel was plunged into bitter war with her neighbours.

Mrs Meir flew to the United States with an urgent request for military assistance to counter the Arab threat. She was granted the assistance she requested.

In October 1973, the Yom Kippur war broke out. Golda Meir spoke of this war as 'a near disaster . . . a nightmare which will always be with me.' The build-up to war had been mounting for months. Egyptian and Syrian troops were massing their troops on Israel's borders. The Israelis, in turn, were reinforcing their own positions. On 5th October—a day before the most important religious holiday in the Jewish calendar, Yom Kippur—Mrs Meir called an emergency meeting of her Cabinet.

Intelligence reports seemed to suggest that trouble was brewing. But the consensus of military opinion was that, although war was imminent, it would not

Confident Israeli troops.

Mrs Meir talks to troops on the Golan Heights with Defence Minister Dyan.

happen for some time. Golda Meir was uneasy, however. Her intuition told her that all was not well. At 4 a.m. the following morning she was woken from a restless sleep by the telephone. Her military secretary told her that information had just been received that the Egyptians and Syrians would launch a joint attack on Israel 'late in the afternoon'.

All over Israel Jews were awakening to spend the holy day at prayer in the synagogues. Soon, thousands of young men would be called up to fight, and once again, the country would be at war.

Military assistance

Mrs Meir held an early morning emergency meeting with her Ministers. The air force chief suggested a pre-emptive strike against the enemy. Mrs Meir rejected the idea because she said it would make Israel the aggressor. Besides, it was a Jewish holy day.

At noon the air raid sirens sounded all over Israel. The war had begun. The country was not prepared for war, and in the first few days Israel seemed to be losing. But the Israelis were prepared to defend their country to the last man and they fought with grim determination. Thousands of lives were lost.

Golda Meir was deeply distressed by the war. She felt guilty at not having obeyed her instincts and ordered a full-scale mobilization which would have given the army time to consolidate its positions.

Urgent messages were sent to the United States requesting military assistance. Fighter planes, tanks, ammunition, medical supplies and rockets poured into the country. The tide turned and Israel managed to push deep into the Arab territories.

The United Nations Security Council, meeting in emergency session, passed a resolution calling for a ceasefire. On the 11th November Israel and Egypt

Golda Meir giving a press conference when she was Prime Minister.

Golda Meir's coffin lies in state in front of the Knesset in 1978.

signed a peace agreement. But peace was still not a reality. There were constant violations of the cease-fire by both sides.

Mrs Meir came under fierce attack in Israel for her role in the Yom Kippur war. She was criticized for making crucial decisions which led to the war, and for not mobilizing the army when it seemed obvious that war would break out. The Labour Party, which she led, was in disarray and she had to struggle to keep an effective government in office.

On the 10th April 1974, she announced she would retire. 'It is beyond my strength to continue carrying this burden,' she said. On the 4th June she left office.

Golda Meir died four years later, at the age of eighty. She had been seriously ill for some years. The 'grandmother' of Israel never lived to see true peace in the country she loved.

Dates and events

1898	Golda Mabovitch born in Kiev, Russia (3rd May).
1905	Family emigrates to America. Golda becomes interested in Zionist movement and joins Labour Zionist Party.
1917	Marries Morris Myerson.
1921	Golda and husband leave America to settle in Palestine where they work on a kibbutz. Golda elected to represent kibbutz on the Council of the Histradruth (Jewish trade union).
1928	Sent to America to build up the Pioneer Women — a fund-raising organization.
1931	Made member of Executive Committee of the Histradruth on return to Palestine.
1946-7	Employed on diplomatic missions by the Jewish Agency.
1947	United Nations votes in favour of partition of Palestine.
1948-9	Golda Meir in Moscow as first Israeli Ambassador.
1948	Creation of the Jewish State — signing of Declaration of Independence (14th May).
1949	Golda Meir enters government as Minister for Labour and Social Security.
1956-65	Serves as Foreign Minister.
1969	Voted Prime Minister (7th March) and subsequently wins general election.
1973	Yom Kippur war (October).
1974	Leads government through long political crisis. Resigns premiership. Left office 14th June.
1978	Golda Meir dies.

Indira Gandhi

The popularity of her father, Jawaharlal Nehru, paved the way for Indira Gandhi's election as Prime Minister of India in 1966. She led her country to a decisive victory in the war against Pakistan. However, accusations of corruption led to her downfall in 1977. She returned to office in 1980 and, despite continued criticism of her dictatorial power, still retains a large and loyal following among the Indian voters.

For more than thirteen years Indira Gandhi has ruled India with an iron hand. Leader of the largest democracy on earth, she is probably the most powerful woman in the world today. Of all the women who have been elected as Prime Minister, Mrs Gandhi is without question the most enigmatic, the most controversial, the most powerful and the most lonely.

From an early age Indira became involved in the Indian political scene as both her father, Jawaharlal Nehru, and her grandfather were deeply committed to the cause of national independence. Born and brought up in a household where political discussions were an intrinsic part of family life, Indira soon came to appreciate the causes for which members of her family were willing to endure imprisonment. Supporting her father during his years as Prime Minister, Indira gained a deep awareness of the delicate problems involved in governing her country. As she emerged from her father's shadow, Indira Gandhi showed she had both the courage and the determination to continue her father's work of building up a strong India. Despite fierce opposition and criticism, she is convinced that she is the only person capable of uniting the diverse Indian peoples and leading them to prosperity and peace.

Indira Priyardarshini ('dear to behold') Nehru was

A street in Allahabad in 1902. Mrs Gandhi was born in this town in 1917.

born on 19th November 1917 at Allahabad in northern India. It was the year of the Russian Revolution and a time, too, of growing restlessness in India. The people had been governed by Britain for more than a hundred years and were growing impatient with the rule of their colonial masters.

Indira's father, Jawaharlal Nehru, and her grandfather, Motilal, were both prominent members of the Indian National Congress—an organization that was dedicated to achieving independence for India. Her mother, Kamala, was also an active member of the organization, as were other members of the family.

Indu, as she was affectionately called, was an only child. She was doted upon by her parents and grandparents. But her childhood was lonely and insecure. She was only four when her father and grandfather were jailed for speaking out against the British. Her mother was also imprisoned a short while afterwards.

The Nehrus were an extremely wealthy family and belonged to the highest caste in India. Jawaharlal had been educated at Harrow and Cambridge and, like his father, was a respected and highly-paid lawyer. The family wore Western clothes and took luxury

Indira with her father and mother, Jawaharlal and Kamala Nehru.

Mahatma Gandhi with his grand-daughters. He was a close friend of the Nehru family.

holidays abroad.

However, by the time Indira was born, the family had rejected this ostentatious lifestyle. This was due to the influence of Mahatma Gandhi—the famous pacifist leader, who, more than any other person, was responsible for bringing about India's freedom. This frail man, who commanded the respect of millions of Indians, had become a close friend of the family. He lived extremely simply and urged the Nehrus to do likewise.

Early political activities

Indira became involved with the independence movement from a very early age. There was a constant stream of political leaders and Congress Party workers in and out of the house. Most of the discussions centred on politics. When she played with her dolls, Indira would make them act out aspects of the fight against the British that she had seen herself or heard her elders describe.

The 1930s were a period of growing conflict with the British, and Indira's father had succeeded her grandfather as President of the Congress Party. Indira wanted to join the Party but she was told she had to wait until she was eighteen.

Indira decided that if she could not join the Party she would set up her own organization, which she called the Monkey Brigade. More than a thousand boys and girls turned up for the inaugural meeting, which was held in the grounds of the Nehrus' home. Indira's family and the British authorities did not take the Monkey Brigade seriously. But, for Indira it was serious work. Under her stern supervision, members of the brigade relieved their elders of such tasks as writing notices, addressing envelopes, making flags, cooking food and supplying drinking water at meetings. They also carried secret

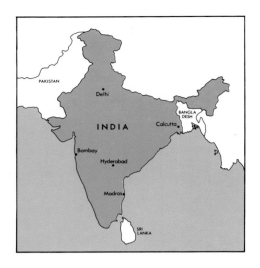

The Indian sub-continent, the largest democracy in the world.

messages and even gathered intelligence about impending police moves.

Indira's father spent more than ten years in jail, much of it in solitary confinement. During these periods of imprisonment, he wrote more than two hundred letters to his daughter on a wide variety of subjects, ranging from the political system in England to the history of China. By writing such letters, her father managed, at least temporarily, to demolish the prison walls that stood between him and his adored child.

Indira inherited her father's love of reading. The library at home contained more than 6,000 books which her father had collected. When she was absorbed in a book, she would often forget to eat or play. Her formal schooling was intermittent and varied. An unsettled family life meant that she was moved from one institution to another, and this contributed to her feelings of insecurity.

Indira leaves for Britain

In 1935, at the age of eighteen, Indira accompanied her mother to Switzerland. Kamala Nehru was suffering from tuberculosis and doctors had advised her to seek medical treatment at a Swiss sanatorium. She died a year later.

A distraught Indira left for Britain to continue her education. Alone in a foreign country Indira drew great comfort and strength from her friendship with Feroze Gandhi whom she had known since childhood. In 1938 she went to Somerville College, Oxford, where she studied public and social administration, history and anthropology, and became a member of the students' wing of the British Labour Party. During the war years Indira enrolled as a Red Cross volunteer and did duty as an ambulance driver.

By 1941, the struggle for Indian independence had

The marriage of Indira Nehru to Feroze Gandhi in Allahabad in 1942.

reached a critical phase. Indira felt she had to be at her father's side. She sailed for India with Feroze Gandhi. A few months after their return Indira and Feroze were married.

Five months later, the Gandhis were in trouble with the British authorities. The Congress Party had started a Quit-India movement, demanding that the British hand over power. As a result the entire Party leadership, including Indira's father and Mahatma Gandhi, were arrested. The country was in turmoil. Official buildings were burned down, railway tracks removed and bridges damaged.

Indira and Feroze are arrested

All political activities had been banned by the British, but undeterred, Indira arranged a meeting of Congress Party workers. When she arrived to speak, the venue was surrounded by policemen carrying guns and long, heavy, steel-studded canes. Indira had been addressing the gathering for no more than a few minutes when a British soldier ordered her to stop. She refused. He then raised his gun and moved menacingly towards her. Feroze, who was in the audience, sprang forward and planted himself between the angry soldier and Indira. A violent scuffle ensued, resulting in the arrest of both Indira and Feroze.

Indira spent eight months in jail. She vowed that she would not allow her jailers or the harsh regulations to get her down and took the deprivations and inconveniences of jail-life in her stride. She had taken a suitcase of books with her and read voraciously. Her experiences in prison, she said, helped her to understand better what her father has endured and 'perhaps it strengthened my character—strengthened me as a person.'

The making of a Prime Minister

Father elected Prime Minister of independent India . . . Becomes father's companion . . . Elected President of Congress Party . . . Husband dies . . . Father dies . . . Withdrawl from public life . . . Return to politics . . . Ministerial posts . . . Defuses rebellion in Madras . . . Foils Pakistani plan to annex Kashmir . . . Prime Minister dies . . . Elected Prime Minister.

When India was at last granted freedom, it came with all the swiftness of a monsoon storm. Churchill and his Tory Party had been defeated in a general election. The new British Prime Minister, Clement Atlee, saw little point in war-enfeebled Britain trying to retain its Empire.

The British Government formally handed over power to India's Constituent Assembly at midnight on 14th August 1947. In a voice choked with emotion, Jawaharlal Nehru, the first Prime Minister of an independent India, declared: 'This is the moment when we step out from the old to the new, when an age ends and when the soul of a nation, long-suppressed, finds utterance.' This was one of the most moving moments in Indira's life.

Four years later, Indira was invited to stand as a candidate in the country's first general election. But she declined the offer. She felt that her father, who was over sixty and lonely and bowed down under the weight of running a country of India's size and problems, needed her help. Jawaharlal Nehru's two most trusted friends and comrades in the freedom struggle were dead. Mahatma Gandhi had been assassinated in 1948, and Vallabhai Patel, the Deputy Prime Minister, had died two years later. Indira Gandhi now became her father's most trusted adviser.

Mrs Gandhi had borne two sons before independence, Rajiv and Sanjay. They were both attending a good private school in New Delhi and were looked after by a European governess. The Gandhis' marriage had begun to disintegrate and the couple saw each other infrequently.

Indira was free to act as her father's household manager, unpaid secretary-cum-nurse, constant companion and conscience-keeper. She was also around when world leaders discussed wide-ranging international issues with him, and was present when Indian politicians brought their problems to him.

Jawaharlal Nehru with his daughter and her two sons, Sanjay and Rajiv.

Indira could not help but collect a rich store of political experience and an understanding of complex international and national affairs. It was the finest political training that a future Prime Minister could have acquired.

Together with her father, she travelled to meet world leaders in China, the Soviet Union, the United States, France and Britain, and attended important conferences. In 1955 Indira was elected to the important Congress Working Committee. It was the first step that ultimately led to her national leadership. Indira's power and influence were growing steadily and in 1959 she was elected President of the Congress Party. A year later, her husband died of a heart attack. The death of Feroze brought Nehru and his daughter even closer together. But time was running out for Nehru. The strain of his lifelong struggle for an independent India, and the pressures in dealing with the country's problems had taken their toll on his health. Jawaharlal Nehru died in 1964. Although Indira knew that his life was drawing

Mrs Gandhi buries documents connected with her father's life. The capsule should remain intact for about a thousand years.

to an end, his death dazed her. Now she stood alone.

Indira went into a period of silent withdrawal after her father's death. She said she wanted to go and live in London to be close to her sons who were studying in England. But, in time, her grief abated. Relatives and family friends urged her not to give up politics. The work that her father had begun—to make India not only free but strong as well—needed her support.

Lal Bahadur Shastri, who had succeeded Nehru as Prime Minister, persuaded Indira to accept the post of Minister of Information and Broadcasting in his government. He also included her in the powerful Emergency Committee of the Cabinet.

Pakistan attacks Kashmir

Seven months after her appointment, the southern state of Madras erupted in a frenzy of lawlessness and rioting. The cause of this revolt was the government's decision to make Hindi the national language of India. The Tamil-speaking southern states feared that this decision would lead to their domination by the Hindi-speaking northern states. Indira, who was herself a Hindi-speaker from the northern state of Uttar Pradesh, unexpectedly took it upon herself to fly to Madras to resolve the issue. To everyone's amazement, she managed to defuse the situation and tempers cooled.

Within months, Indira found herself involved in an even bigger crisis. She had gone to Kashmir—the Nehrus' ancestral homeland—at the beginning of August 1965 for a brief holiday. Her arrival in Srinagar, the state's capital, coincided with the beginning of a Pakistani attack on Kashmir. This culminated four weeks later in a full-scale war between India and Pakistan. Several thousand Pakistani soldiers had infiltrated Kashmir disguised as tribal raiders. The Pakistani government had hoped

Indira Gandhi addresses a group of Congress Party members.

to catch the Indian security forces unawares and capture the coveted territory with the help of local sympathizers.

When Indira's plane landed at Srinagar, the raiders were only a few miles from the capital and were moving purposefully towards the airport which they hoped to capture. Indira was advised to fly back to Delhi immediately. But she declined and instead drove directly to the military control room that had been hastily established.

The military and political leaders were impressed by the firm and courageous way in which Mrs Gandhi handled the situation. Her instinctive assessment of the magnitude of the Pakistani threat proved to be more accurate than that of the military or the Central Intelligence Bureau. Indira kept in constant touch with the Prime Minister about the situation and attended the emergency meetings of the state government. By the end of her 'holiday' the Pakistani plan to annex Kashmir had been foiled.

Shastri, too, was impressed by Indira's handling of the crisis. But he saw in her a potential threat to his power. Shortly after he had become Prime Minister, she had attacked him for abandoning her late father's policies and programmes. As a result, Shastri tried to isolate her and seldom consulted her on important official or party matters. Other politicians began to drift away from her and she felt increasingly neglected and bitter.

Her fortunes were to change dramatically, however. In January 1966, Shastri flew to the Soviet city of Tashkent to negotiate a peace treaty with Pakistan. He died of heart failure a few hours after signing the controversial and important agreement.

The news of Shastri's death reached the Indian capital at 3 a.m. Within hours, a small group of friends had assembled at Indira's home. Mrs Gandhi declared herself willing to stand for election as the new Prime Minister.

The two main contenders for the post, Morarji Desai, and G. L. Nanda, who had become acting Prime Minister, were hungry for power. But the President of the Congress Party decided that Indira was the only person capable of uniting a sufficient number of M.P.s behind her. He managed to get the chief ministers of ten states to endorse his decision. Nanda decided to quit the race. It was now a straight fight between Mrs Gandhi and Desai.

It took nearly four hours for the 526 members of the Congress Party in the two houses of Parliament to cast their votes. Thousands of Indians had gathered outside the circular, red-stone Parliament House to hear the results of the fight. When it was announced, they broke into excited cheering—Mrs Gandhi had secured 355 votes against Desai's 169. It was a decisive victory and India had made history in electing its first woman Prime Minister.

Indira Gandhi casting her vote at Parliament House in New Delhi.

The most powerful woman in the world

In her first few months as Prime Minister, Indira Gandhi proved that she was a force to be reckoned with. She gained universal admiration and respect among the ordinary people, many of whom worshipped her as a virtual goddess.

But she also made countless enemies. The men who had been left out of her Cabinet were jealous and angry. They were determined to get their revenge. The newspapers ran stories questioning whether she had the necessary qualities to rule the country. They pointed out her lack of administrative experience and inadequate grasp of financial and economic complexities.

Indira Gandhi was under considerable strain, and she often appeared tense and irritable. But, in time, she proved that she had tremendous personal courage, a will to rule and a sharp eye for the weaknesses of her opponents.

She initiated a programme of drastic reforms and declared war on India's endemic disease of corruption. High officials were arrested for smuggling and she began an ambitious programme designed to set the nation's economy on an even keel.

General election campaign

Mrs Gandhi faced her first general election a year after her election as Prime Minister. It was a long and bitter campaign. She travelled more than 56,000 kilometres (35,000 miles)—many of it by jeep over rough roads—to address rallies in various parts of the country. Wherever she went, she drew large crowds. Often she would be shouted at by hostile elements in the audience. But she faced them undaunted and the sometimes ugly confrontations usually ended in her victory.

On one occasion, an angry group began pelting her with stones. She was hit in the face, but she went

Indira Gandhi speaking at an election rally.

ahead with her speech despite a fairly nasty injury. The sight of her speaking while stemming the flow of blood with her sari shamed the hecklers into silence and awed the crowd. Like her father, Indira was at her best when challenged. She discovered that she had also inherited his capacity to be stimulated by contact with the masses.

Despite her vigorous campaigning, the Congress Party fared badly in the elections, scraping through to victory by only a narrow margin. Morarji Desai, her rival for the Party leadership at the time of Shastri's death, declared that Indira was to blame for the Congress Party's poor showing at the polls. He said she was 'unfit' to be Prime Minister and that the party should elect him for the job. However, Mrs Gandhi proved to be a shrewd tactician. She offered him the job of Deputy Prime Minister and Finance Minister. Desai gave up his attacks, having realized that his chances of becoming Prime Minister were diminishing.

In the following months Mrs Gandhi consolidated her power. She announced that the banks would be

The President's residence in Delhi.

nationalized. The 'Old Guard' in the Congress Party, led by Desai, were stunned by her decision. Many of them had vested interests in the banks, and would lose a lot of money as a result of Mrs Gandhi's decision. Mr Desai resigned his post.

In the elections of 1971, the people of India gave Mrs Gandhi's party an overwhelming majority in Parliament. Her rivals in the party had been eliminated and none dared challenge her authority. Overseas newspapers referred to her as 'The Most Powerful Woman in the World' and 'The Empress of India'.

Mrs Gandhi, accompanied by Harold Macmillan, receiving a degree at Oxford University.

The Pakistani threat

Mrs Gandhi faced the gravest challenge of her life in the twelve months following her victory at the polls. The threat came from Pakistan, India's neighbour and old adversary. The Hindu population of East Pakistan were demanding autonomy from Moslem-dominated West Pakistan. The Pakistani Army began a vicious crackdown on the Hindu people, and thousands were tortured and killed.

Millions of East Pakistanis fled to India to escape the brutal repression. When the flood of refugees had reached nine million, Mrs Gandhi declared: 'We have no intention of absorbing these people here.' India was forced to spend more than £3 million a day on feeding the refugees. China and the West supported the military junta in Pakistan. India signed a treaty with Moscow whereby the Soviet Union promised to aid the country in the event of war. It was a dangerous time in world affairs. Indira Gandhi visited the major world leaders and urged them to put pressure on Pakistan to end the bloodshed, but to no avail.

On the morning of 3rd December 1971, Pakistan Air Force planes attacked Indian Air Force Stations.

Indian males wait to be sterilized. Family planning was encouraged by Mrs Gandhi's government.

At 10 p.m. Mrs Gandhi announced that India was at war with Pakistan. The war was short and bloody, ending in a decisive victory for India. It also resulted in the creation of the independent state of East Pakistan, which was soon renamed Bangladesh.

Indira Gandhi's popularity soared as a result of her charismatic leadership during the war with Pakistan. She was portrayed as a woman with uncommon practical sense and a capacity for purposeful and ruthless action. She was acclaimed as a heroine and even her most vehement critics admitted a grudging respect for her.

'Black money'

But the euphoria faded a few months after India's victory. Mrs Gandhi's popularity began to decline, as she began to assume dictatorial powers. Her critics accused her of corruption, callous misuse of authority, and a sharp decline in administrative efficiency.

The government was rocked by a series of scandals. The first involved the enormous amounts of 'black money' that the Congress Party had allegedly collected from big businesses and industrialists to fund its election campaign. 'Black money' is the term used to describe cash on which no tax has been paid.

The other major scandal centred around the activities of her younger, and favourite son Sanjay, who had become an increasingly powerful political figure. He had been put in charge of reorganizing the youth section of the Congress Party, and enjoyed Indira's full support. Sanjay was a ruthless, aggressive and arrogant man. He had studied automobile engineering in Britain, and on his return to India, planned to produce a small car for the Indian masses. Many questioned how Sanjay managed to acquire factory premises and the necessary capital for his scheme so

Sanjay, Mrs Gandhi's younger son. His plans for compulsory sterilization were unpopular.

easily. The Opposition insisted that Mrs Gandhi had used her power and influence to help Sanjay. She denied the charge. Sanjay's venture ultimately proved a costly failure.

But this scandal was a storm in a teacup, compared with what was to come. The Indian government, on Sanjay's insistence, had embarked on a programme of forcible sterilization in an attempt to slow down the country's massive birth rate. Sanjay insisted that compulsory sterilization was absolutely necessary for the economic development of India. The plan met with massive resistance and led to widespread rioting.

Sanjay also persuaded his mother to embark on a massive slum clearance campaign in the larger Indian cities of Bombay and Calcutta. Police and army units stood by while bulldozers razed homes to the ground, often with the residents or their possessions still inside. The slum dwellers were bitter and angry. They did not want to live in slums, but the government had demolished their homes without providing alternative accommodation. Sanjay insisted that they would have to move out of the cities and into the rural areas.

Indira's rule as dictator

Sanjay's manipulation of power caused deep resentment, and together with a variety of other economic and social problems led to increasing opposition to Mrs Gandhi and her rule. There were widespread strikes and riots.

Mrs Gandhi's response was to declare a State of Emergency and she began her rule as dictator. Thousands of her opponents were imprisoned without trial and the Press was heavily censored.

The State of Emergency ended as abruptly as it had begun. Mrs Gandhi announced that a general

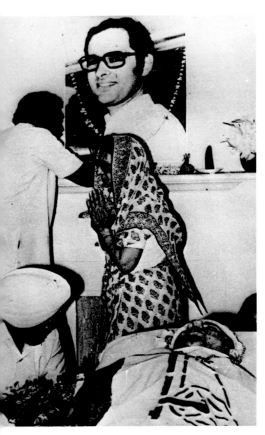

Mrs Gandhi beside the body of Sanjay, after he had been killed in a plane crash in 1980.

election would be held in March 1977 in the belief that the 650 million people of India would support her. But she had seriously misjudged the mood of the electorate and her Party was thrashed at the polls. Mrs Gandhi was imprisoned for a brief period and was threatened with criminal proceedings concerning electoral malpractice and bribery.

Her arch-opponent, Morarji Desai, became the new Prime Minister. For Mrs Gandhi, her defeat was a bitter and humiliating blow.

The return to power

For two and a half years she was a political outcast. Then in the elections of January 1980 Mrs Gandhi led her Congress Party back to a stunning victory and once again became Prime Minister. The thousands of Indians who lined the streets to welcome her back to power cried out in chorus 'Indira Gandhi ki jai'—long live Indira Gandhi.

Six months after returning to power, Mrs Gandhi suffered a severe personal tragedy. Sanjay, whom she had assiduously groomed as her potential successor, died in a plane crash a few hundred yards from her home. Mrs Gandhi rushed to the scene, but Sanjay and his passenger had been killed on impact. The Prime Minister was shocked and grief-stricken. To honour her son, she commissioned the building of a huge pavilion, which was filled with thousands of photographs of Sanjay.

Sanjay's elder brother, Rajiv, was seen as Mrs Gandhi's natural successor. A quiet, serious man who has declared that he is 'not really interested in politics', Rajiv is completely different from Sanjay. Nevertheless, he has come to his mother's aid as an adviser and has urged her to use her power wisely. It remains to be seen whether Rajiv has the ability to persuade his mother to follow his moderate advice.

Since returning to power, Mrs Gandhi has re-introduced some of the draconian legislation of the emergency period to deal with growing lawlessness, strikes and savage conflicts between Hindus and Moslems. Despite the numerous problems that beset India, Mrs Gandhi commands immense popularity. In 1981, more than two million Indians attended a political rally in New Delhi to demonstrate their support for her. But in the uncertain, fast-changing world of Indian politics, Mrs Gandhi could once again find herself out of power.

Dates and events

1917　Indira Priyardarshini Nehru born in Allahabad, India (19th November).

1935　Accompanies mother to Switzerland.

1938　Following her mother's death, Indira goes to England. Studies at Somerville College, Oxford.

1939　Joins Indian Congress Party.

1941　Returns to India to support father, Jawaharlal Nehru, in his struggle to establish Indian independence.

1942　Marries Feroze Gandhi. Indira and her husband imprisoned for defying ban on political meetings during Quit-India campaign.

1947　India granted independence (14th August).

1951　Indira Gandhi invited to stand as candidate in country's first general election. Declines offer.

1955　Elected to Congress Working Committee.

1959　Elected as President of the Congress Party.

1960　Feroze Gandhi dies.

1964　Jawaharlal Nehru dies. Indira Gandhi accepts post of Minister of Information and Broadcasting in new government led by Lal Shastri.

1966　Elected as Prime Minister (24th January) following Shastri's sudden death.

1967　Wins general election by narrow margin. Announces plans to nationalize banks despite fierce opposition.

1971　Returned to power in general election by overwhelming majority. Thirteen-day war with Pakistan (December). Seeks to control Indian birth rate by introducing birth control and forcible sterilization. Growing influence of her younger son, Sanjay.

1974　Growing unrest in country due to economic and social problems.

1975　State of Emergency declared.

1977　Mrs Gandhi and Congress Party suffer heavy defeat in general election.

1980　Leads Congress Party back to power. Death of Sanjay in plane crash.

Margaret Thatcher

'The most unpopular woman in Britain' is just one of the many nicknames of Margaret Thatcher —the first woman Prime Minister of a European country. Her tough and uncompromising stand on many issues has gained her many admirers, both at home and abroad, and also many critics. Despite rising unemployment, she has continued to implement controversial policies in an effort to restore Britain's economic stability.

Margaret Thatcher—the 'Iron Lady' of British politics—came to power at a time when Britain was going through its most severe economic crisis since the Second World War. This passionate and determined woman, who rose from humble origins to become the country's first woman Prime Minister, has vowed to put Britain on her feet again.

Mrs Thatcher's rise to power was dramatic. Before February 1975, nobody in Britain seriously believed that a woman would ever become leader of the traditionally-minded Conservative Party. But, against all the odds and predictions of political commentators, this ambitious and hard-headed politician achieved what many had thought impossible. As leader of the Tories, Margaret Thatcher led her party to victory in the general election of 1979 and became the first woman Prime Minister of a European country.

History will judge whether Mrs Thatcher's attempts to radically change British society have been a success or a failure. A forceful and controversial politician, Margaret Thatcher inspires wrath in her critics and adulation in her supporters. Her opponents say she is an authoritarian, demonic Right-wing reactionary who is leading the country on the road to disaster. Her admirers view her as a compassionate, sincere and courageous woman who

Margaret Thatcher (right) with her parents and elder sister, Muriel, in 1945.

is dedicated to restoring the strength of Britain's economy.

Margaret Hilda Roberts was born on the morning of 13th October 1925 in the flat above her parents' grocery shop in Grantham, a small market town in the heart of the Lincolnshire countryside.

Alfred Roberts and his wife Beatrice were an intensely religious and hard-working couple and from an early age, Margaret and her elder sister Muriel were subjected to a rigid discipline.

Early political education

Alfred Roberts was a Methodist lay preacher and an active member of the local council and a variety of voluntary organizations. He later became Mayor of Grantham and sat as a J.P. on the local bench. Her father exercised a tremendous influence on Margaret. 'We were Methodists, and Methodist means method. We were taught what was right and wrong in very considerable detail. He never tolerated the words "I can't" or "It's too difficult" and constantly drummed into me, from a very early age, "You make up your own mind. You do not follow the crowd because you are afraid of being different—you decide what to do yourself and if necessary you lead the crowd, but you never just follow." Oh that was very hard indeed but my goodness it has stood me in good stead.'

Margaret and her sister were expected to help out in the shop from an early age. This is where Margaret's political education first began as she listened to her father discussing political topics with the customers. As she grew older, she took a more active interest in the discussions and often made her own pertinent contributions.

She did well at primary school and won a scholarship to the Kesteven and Grantham Girls' School

After leaving university, Margaret Thatcher joined a firm in Essex as a research chemist.

when she was ten, a year younger than normal. Margaret failed to come top of the class in only one of the seven years of her school career. She also took an active part in school drama productions and the debating society, and played centre-half for the hockey team. Margaret's classmates remember her as a rather serious and hard-working girl.

She was very ambitious and had set her sights on Oxford where she wanted to study chemistry. However, Latin was not taught at her school and she had to pass an examination in Latin before she could be admitted to Oxford. Against the advice of her headmistress, she crammed a five-year course of Latin into one year with the help of a tutor and came first in the examination.

Student life at Oxford

In 1943 Margaret won a bursary to Somerville College, Oxford and, after an initial period of homesickness, settled into student life. She worked hard but also found time to sing in the Bach Choir and worked, twice a week, in the Oxford forces canteen. For the first time in her life she was able to go out dancing.

It was wartime, and the prevailing political fashion at Oxford was socialism—a philosophy that she has vehemently opposed all her life. She joined the Conservative Club and later became President of the Oxford University Conservative Association. Margaret worked hard for the Association, organizing numerous meetings, debates and speeches. Leading politicians were invited from Westminster to address the students. Margaret canvassed in Oxford during the post-war election campaign, and also made a number of speeches in her home town in support of the Conservative candidate.

The overwhelming defeat of the Conservative

Mrs Thatcher canvassing in Dartford during the elections in 1951.

Government at the polls in 1945 came as an unexpected and shattering blow to the Tory Party, and Margaret, like many other Tories, was distressed by the result.

It was at that time that the idea of making a career for herself in politics first occurred to Margaret. However, she was still studying and knew that her priority, on leaving university, would be to earn her living. Margaret graduated from Oxford with a second class honours degree in chemistry and in 1947 went to work for a plastics firm at Manningtree, Essex.

Margaret's first Party conference

Although she was interested in her job and got on well with her colleagues, Margaret's over-riding interest was politics. She joined the local Conservative Association and in 1948 went to her first Party conference as a representative of the Oxford Graduates' Association.

At the conference, a close friend of Margaret's was sitting next to the chairman of the Dartford constituency. The man mentioned that they were looking for a candidate for the forthcoming election. Margaret's friend asked if he would consider a woman. 'Oh no,' came the immediate answer, 'not a woman.' But after meeting Margaret Roberts, the chairman urged her to put her name down as a contender.

In those days, it was much more difficult for a woman to get into politics than it is now. There were twenty-six other candidates and Margaret was the only woman. But she was unanimously adopted by the Dartford selection committee and, at twenty-four, became the youngest woman candidate in the country.

Margaret campaigned energetically, and managed

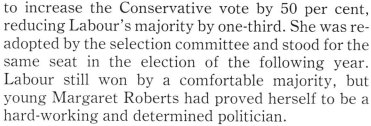

An engagement photograph of Margaret Roberts and her future husband, Denis Thatcher.

Norman Dodds receives Margaret Thatcher's congratulations after winning Dartford in 1951.

to increase the Conservative vote by 50 per cent, reducing Labour's majority by one-third. She was re-adopted by the selection committee and stood for the same seat in the election of the following year. Labour still won by a comfortable majority, but young Margaret Roberts had proved herself to be a hard-working and determined politician.

It was while she was fighting the Dartford seat in 1950 that Margaret met Denis Thatcher. They married on 13th December 1951 and two years later Margaret Thatcher gave birth to twins, Mark and Carol. Denis Thatcher had inherited a successful paint company from his father and was able to support his wife and children very comfortably.

Mrs Thatcher, who had enrolled as a law student at Lincoln's Inn before her marriage, continued her studies and employed a nanny to look after the twins. She practised for five years as a barrister, specializing in taxation law.

Margaret Thatcher was determined to get elected to Parliament, and maintained her interest in politics while practising as a lawyer. She tried on two occasions to be selected as a candidate, and at the third attempt was adopted for Finchley—a safe Conservative seat. She won the seat in 1959 by a comfortable margin and realized her ambition to get into Parliament.

Britain's first woman Prime Minister

Margaret Thatcher entered Parliament on 20th October 1959. Not even in her wildest dreams, or her most ambitious moments, could she have foreseen the developments that lay ahead in her political career.

Within a few months she had become a prominent member of a group of Conservative M.P.s who were demanding the reinstatement of corporal punishment for young offenders. Mrs Thatcher was dubbed a 'Right-wing reactionary', but the title did not seem to bother her.

In 1961 Mrs Thatcher was promoted to the post of Joint Parliamentary Secretary to the Ministry of Pensions and National Insurance. She remained in this post until the Conservative Government suffered defeat in the 1964 General Election. Mrs Thatcher managed to retain her seat against strong opposition from the Liberals, but her majority was nearly halved.

Minister of Education

Between 1964 and 1970, when the Labour Party was in power, Margaret Thatcher gained a wide range of experience as Opposition spokesman on a variety of subjects. In 1967 she was promoted to the Shadow Cabinet as spokesman on Fuel and Power and became Shadow Minister of Transport in a later reshuffle. In 1969 Mrs Thatcher was made Shadow Minister of Education, and was later appointed Minister of Education when the Conservatives won the 1970 General Election.

It was as Minister of Education that Margaret Thatcher became what the *Sun* newspaper described as 'The most unpopular woman in Britain'. Her attitudes on educational policy aroused a great deal of controversy and she met with fierce opposition from the Press, teachers and students.

The Minister of Education at work in her office.

Students demonstrating for increased grants.

The first confrontation between the new Minister and her critics came shortly after her appointment. She announced in Parliament that free school milk for the over-sevens was to be abolished, and that school meal charges were to be increased. These measures were implemented to save £52 million on the Education Budget. Outraged protests followed the announcement. Overnight, she became known as 'Thatcher—the Milk Snatcher' and she became the target of a prolonged campaign of hostility.

During her four years as Minister of Education she was dogged by controversy. It seemed that she could satisfy nobody. She was snubbed by teachers' representatives at important functions and encountered hostile demonstrations from students.

Contender for Party leadership

In 1974 Mrs Thatcher found herself on the Opposition benches when the Conservative Government, under the leadership of Edward Heath, was defeated in the general election. However, within a few months she was once again making headlines—this time as contender for the leadership of the Conservative Party.

Mrs Thatcher and other M.P.s on the Right wing of the Party were determined to topple Edward Heath, who had lost three elections out of his four during his time as Leader. The main Right-wing contender for the leadership was Sir Keith Joseph, who was a close friend and ally of Mrs Thatcher. She said she would not stand for election if Sir Keith was a candidate, as she felt that the traditionally-minded Conservative Party was not yet ready for a woman leader.

Luck was on her side, however. Sir Keith made a highly controversial speech in which he suggested that free contraceptives should be issued to reduce the number of unwanted children borne by young

Sir Keith Joseph addresses the Conservative Party conference in 1977.

unmarried, working-class mothers. His remarks caused a furore and he was forced to drop out of the leadership battle.

With Sir Keith out of the running, Mrs Thatcher declared that she would stand for the leadership. Not many people took her challenge seriously at first. But, as the day of the first ballot for the leadership election drew near, her opponents began to get worried.

February 4th 1975 had been chosen as the day for the first ballot. There were only three candidates: Edward Heath, Margaret Thatcher and Hugh Fraser. The Press had predicted that Mr Heath would emerge as victor by a clear margin, so it came as a bombshell when the result of the ballot was announced. Mrs Thatcher had obtained 130 votes to Mr Heath's 119. Hugh Fraser trailed far behind with only 16 votes. A shattered Mr Heath—the first Tory leader to be dethroned against his will in more than 50 years—announced his resignation on the early evening news.

It was not the end of the battle. There was to be a second ballot a week later. There were five candidates for the second round, but Mrs Thatcher won by

Margaret Thatcher after winning the Tory Party leadership elections in 1974.

Margaret Thatcher with members of her Shadow Cabinet in 1975.

a wide margin. On hearing the result, she said, 'Thank God it was decisive. We have got a lot to do. Now we must get down to work at once.'

Mrs Thatcher was radiant in victory and her supporters were ecstatic. The reaction of the Press, the public and politicians varied from delight to cautious scepticism. But even her most ardent critics had to concede that she had displayed 'courage and guts' in entering the leadership battle.

For Margaret Thatcher, her election as the first ever woman leader of the traditionally-minded Conservative Party marked a decisive turning point in her political career. When she was formally adopted as the leader of the party a few days after the ballot, she gave a rousing speech in which she promised to do her utmost to lead the Conservatives to victory at the next election.

Leader of the Opposition

Mrs Thatcher quickly implemented plans to preserve and consolidate her position, and a number of leading moderates were axed from the Shadow Cabinet. Mr Heath—who had flown to Spain for a holiday after his humiliating defeat—was offered a position in her Shadow Cabinet. Understandably, he declined.

As Leader of the Opposition, Mrs Thatcher made several major tours overseas, visiting the United States, Canada, Australia, New Zealand, India, Pakistan, China, Japan and Hong Kong. She also visited several European and Middle Eastern countries and made contact with important national leaders, politicians and diplomats.

At home, she led the Opposition attack on the faltering Labour Government in the House of Commons, and concentrated on building up the Party's strength ready for when it would face a

James Callaghan's Labour Government was toppled by Mrs Thatcher's vote of No Confidence in Parliament.

general election.

The Labour Government, led by Mr James Callaghan, was beseiged with problems. Rising prices, inflation, strikes, increasing unemployment and the decline of British industry dominated the headlines. By mid-1978 speculation was rife that Mr Callaghan would be forced to call an early election. But, to everyone's surprise, the Prime Minister announced that he had decided to soldier on.

The events of the next few months were crucial in shaping the issues that would determine the result of the election. The new year ushered in a wave of industrial unrest. Hospitals, schools and public services were hit by a spate of strikes, described as the worst since 1926. The crisis became known as the 'winter of discontent'.

In March 1979 Mrs Thatcher announced that she would table a motion of No Confidence in the government. On the 28th March the House of Commons was packed with M.P.s. The atmosphere was electric.

Motion of No Confidence

Mrs Thatcher walked in at precisely 3 p.m. and took her seat opposite Mr Callaghan. She rose to table her motion of No Confidence and spoke for half an hour, ending with these words: 'The only way to renew the authority of parliamentary government is to seek a fresh mandate from the people, and to seek it quickly. I challenge the Government to do so before the day is through.'

Mr Callaghan rose to reply and, in a scathing attack, said that Mrs Thatcher was offering the country nothing more than outdated policies which were doomed to failure.

At 10 p.m. M.P.s streamed back into the lobby to cast their votes. Eighteen minutes later the result was announced—the Government had been defeated

Margaret Thatcher outside 10 Downing Street after winning the 1979 General Election.

by just one vote. It was a narrow, but decisive victory, and the Tories erupted into loud, ecstatic cheers. Mr Callaghan had become the first Prime Minister to be driven out of office and forced into a general election since 1924.

Two days after her victory in the Commons tragedy struck, when Mr Airey Neave was killed in a car-bomb explosion as he was leaving the Houses of Parliament. Airey Neave had not only been a friend and confidant of Mrs Thatcher, but he had also been responsible for her successful campaign to win the leadership of the Conservative Party. His death was a bitter blow for Mrs Thatcher. She once said that she had been taught never to show her emotions in public. But she could not disguise her grief or hold back her tears on that day.

Prime Minister

The date for the election was announced a few days after Mr Neave's death. The nation would go to the polls on 3rd May 1979. In a pre-election address, Margaret Thatcher warned the British people that they faced one of the most crucial periods in history. Her party, she said, offered the country its last chance to 'turn the tide against socialism'. A vote for the Tories, she said, would offer Britain the opportunity to renew its economic and military power.

In the early hours of the morning of 4th May, Mrs Thatcher learned that the electorate had given her an overwhelming vote of confidence—the Conservatives had won an overall majority of forty-four seats in the House of Commons. Margaret Thatcher was exuberant in her triumph. A few hours later, she was driven to Buckingham Palace and then on to No. 10 Downing Street, where a large crowd had gathered to catch a glimpse of Britain's, and Europe's, first woman Prime Minister.

The rule of the 'Iron Lady'

Sets forth the aims of the new government . . . Announces public spending cuts . . . Proposed cutbacks arouse anger of Opposition and trade unions . . . Street marches in protest at cuts . . . Government undeterred . . . Mrs Thatcher and Lord Carrington seek an end to the war in Zimbabwe . . . Peace successfully negotiated at Lancaster House talks . . . Growing opposition to government at home.

Margaret Thatcher wasted no time in implementing her plans to 'turn the tide against socialism'. Within days of taking office, the Conservative Government announced an immediate wage increase for the police and armed forces. Political observers interpreted this as a shrewd tactical move on Mrs Thatcher's part. The government was committed to a programme of radical change, which could possibly lead to outbreaks of civil disorder, and it needed the full backing of the police and armed forces.

In Parliament, Mrs Thatcher announced an ambitious programme of legislation to bring about the changes she thought were necessary to put the country back on its feet. The main aims of the government would be to reduce government spending on health services, housing, social security and education; strengthen the country's military might; curb the power of the trade unions; reduce the flow of immigration; bring down inflation; reverse the decline in British industry; and reduce taxation —particularly for the upper income groups.

Mrs Thatcher's warning

The government's proposals were warmly welcomed in some quarters, particularly by big business corporations and industry. But the Opposition, trade unions and other groups vigorously opposed what they described as 'a savage attack on the Welfare State.' They declared that they would fight Mrs Thatcher every step of the way.

The 'Iron Lady' was unmoved by her critics' attacks. The path ahead would not be easy, she warned, but the country was 'sick and it needed a dose of strong medicine.' The people of Britain, said Mrs Thatcher, had demanded 'better housing, better health services, better social services, better education, better everything, regardless of where the

Mrs Thatcher meeting crowds in Downing Street on the first day of her premiership.

money to pay for it was to come from.'

The government's spending cuts aroused bitter anger. Hospital wards were forced to close, school meals in some areas were stopped and libraries were forced to reduce their staff. Mrs Thatcher was labelled a 'cold-blooded and heartless woman'. Thousands of people took to the streets to march in protest against the cuts, but Mrs Thatcher was undeterred. No one, she said, enjoyed implementing unpopular measures, but the cuts were absolutely necessary.

Mrs Thatcher's critics felt that the government's policies were designed to benefit the rich at the expense of the poor. They pointed out that while the government was making huge cuts in essential services it was spending millions of pounds on nuclear weapons.

The one spectacular success of Mrs Thatcher's early premiership was her decisive role in helping to end the war in Zimbabwe. Ever since Ian Smith's rebel government had announced a Unilateral Declaration of Independence in 1965 thus breaking links with Britain, Rhodesia (as it was then known) had proved a major headache to successive British governments. Britain had been forced to apply economic sanctions against Rhodesia in an effort to

The Houses of Parliament in London.

force the white-led regime to grant political rights to the black majority. The country was ravaged by civil war and thousands of people were killed.

Mrs Thatcher and her Foreign Minister, Lord Carrington, decided that the time had come to solve the problem once and for all. They travelled to the neighbouring country of Zambia and spoke to the leaders of the guerrilla armies. As a result of their initiative, the historic Lancaster House Conference was convened in Britain. Representatives of the black guerrilla armies and of the Rhodesian Government had talks at the conference and it was agreed to hold elections in the country under British supervision. The election resulted in a massive victory for the black nationalist leader, Mr Robert Mugabe.

Criticism from pressure groups

But at home things were not so rosy. The government faced increasing pressure from the trade unions who were demanding higher wage settlements. There was also mounting criticism from a wide variety of pressure groups about the 'savage' nature of the government's spending cuts.

On her first day in office, Mrs Thatcher had expressed the aspirations of her government in the paraphrased words of St. Francis of Assisi:

> *'Where there is discord, may we bring harmony*
> *Where there is error, may we bring truth*
> *Where there is doubt, may we bring faith*
> *Where there is despair, may we bring hope.'*

But after more than two years under the leadership of the 'Iron Lady', Britain was experiencing the ravaging effects of one of the worst economic recessions of the century. Almost three million people were unemployed and there were fears that the nation was heading for social and economic catastrophe. The trade unions and a number of

The Lancaster House Conference in 1979, convened to settle the problem of Rhodesia.

prominent businessmen warned Mrs Thatcher that the country would be economically ruined if she persisted in pursuing her tough economic policies. But she defiantly insisted that, despite rising unemployment and the closure of thousands of businesses, the government was determined to press on with its effort to bring down inflation.

The pressures on Mrs Thatcher are immense. But, once she has made up her mind to follow a particular course of action she is not easily deflected from her aim. 'No great goal was ever easily achieved,' she once said, 'but it is because I care passionately about the future of our country that I am resolved to go on striving.'

Dates and events

1925 Margaret Hilda Roberts born in Grantham, Lincolnshire (13th October).

1935 Wins scholarship to Kesteven and Grantham Girls' School.

1943-7 Studies chemistry at Somerville College, Oxford. Joins Conservative Club and becomes President of the Oxford University Conservative Association.

1947 First job as research assistant for plastics firm at Manningtree, Essex.

1948 Attends her first Conservative Party Conference.

1949 Adopted as Conservative candidate for Dartford.

1950 Enrols as law student at Lincoln's Inn.

1951 Marries Denis Thatcher.

1954 Practises as barrister in London.

1958 Adopted as Conservative candidate for Finchley.

1959 Wins Finchley seat and becomes an M.P. (October).

1961 Appointed Joint Parliamentary Secretary to the Ministry of Pensions and National Insurance.

1964 Defeat of Conservative Government in general election.

1967 Promoted to Shadow Cabinet as Spokesman on Fuel and Power.

1968 Becomes Shadow Minister of Transport.

1969 Becomes Shadow Minister of Education.

1970 Conservatives win general election. Margaret Thatcher becomes Minister of Education.

1974 Tories defeated in general election.

1975 Challenges Party leadership. Becomes first woman leader of the Conservative Party (February).

1979 Tables motion of No Confidence in Labour Government (March). Government defeated and forced to declare general election. Conservatives win general election by majority of 44 seats (3rd May). Margaret Thatcher becomes Britain's first woman Prime Minister. Announces controversial public spending cuts.

1980 Lancaster House talks end in resolution of Rhodesia problem.

Glossary

Annex To take over another country, usually by force.

Assassination The killing of someone treacherously, usually for political motives.

Caste A social class in India.

Civic rights The rights a person has to take part in the running of his country or city.

Clandestine An act done in secrecy.

Democracy Government by the people or their elected representatives.

Dictator A ruler with absolute power, who usually suppresses democracy.

Guerrilla warfare Illegal opposition to a government by small units of armed men.

Holocaust The destruction of people or buildings, especially by fire.

Insurrection A rebellion against the government.

Motion of No Confidence A vote in Parliament challenging a government's policies.

Nationalization The take-over of a firm by a government.

Nepotism Showing favouritism to a relative in politics, etc.

Pacifist A person who opposes the use of violence in settling disputes.

Pogrom An organized massacre of people, especially of Jews.

Pressure group A group organized to influence government policy in a specific area.

Reactionary A person who opposes social or political change.

Republic A democratic system of government, where the head of state is an elected president.

Socialism An economic system in which the means of production and distribution are owned by the State.

State of Emergency Period during which a government has special powers to deal with strikes, a war, etc.

Sterilization To remove a person's ability to reproduce.

Tuberculosis A disease of the lungs.

Zionism The movement to set up a Jewish nation in Palestine.

Further reading

Politics in Sri Lanka: 1945-1973 by A. Jeyaratnam Wilson (St. Martin's Press, 1974)

Indira Gandhi: A Biography by Zareer Masani T. Y. Crowell, 1976)

Indira Gandhi: A Personal and Political Biography by Anand Mohan (Meredith Press, 1967)

Golda: The Uncrowned Queen of Israel by Robert Slater (Jonathan David, 1981)

Golda by William Gibson (Atheneum, 1978)

Madam Prime Minister: Margaret Thatcher and Her Rise to Power by Allan J. Mayer (Newsweek Books, 1979)

Margaret Thatcher: First Lady of the House by Ernie Money (International Publications Service, 1975)

Index

Picture acknowledgements

The publisher would like to thank all those who provided illustrations on the following pages: J. Allan Cash Ltd. 21, 40 (bottom); Alan Hutchison Library 60; Keystone Press Agency *front cover*, 10 (top and bottom), 33, 36, 38, 43, 48, 49, 53 (top), 54 (top), 55, 56, 61; London Express News and Feature Services 26 (bottom); Photri 37, 40 (top); Popperfoto 6 (bottom), 16 (top and bottom), 17, 23, 25 (top and bottom), 31, 35, 41, 42, 53 (bottom), 59; John Topham Picture Library 7, 8 , 12, 27, 30 (top and bottom), 44, 50, 51 (top and bottom); Malcolm S. Walker 4, 6 (top), 9, 13, 14, 28, 32, 46, 54 (bottom), 57.